Table of Contents

Carte Blanche Within

Unleashed Nirvana

Unleashed Nirvana 2

Happiness Is

I Love Him

Reveal Yourself

My Newest Angel

My Light 2

Enlightenment 2

Timeless

Finally

Finally 2

Guiding Light 2

Alluring Skies

My Patch of Old Snow 2

The Power of a Poet

The Power of the Pen

The Power of an Artist

Let's Dance

The Power of Dance

Changing

The Power of the Mic

Affirmations

Caged Bird Once

King

Nubian King

Nubian Queen

My Gift

Vows of Life

Stars 2

Men Are

Women Are

Take My Hand   Vow to My Future Husband

I am

Blue Skies 2   No More Makeup   I'm Worthy

Protect Me   Premonitions or Dreams Waves 2

Prove To Me   Liberate(Free)

Carte Blanche Within

Carte Blanche symbolizes,
freedom, within,
us all,
that illuminates out,
to each one of us.

Individually our Carte Blanche,
ignites a spontaneous spark,
of hope and Carte Blanche.

Encircling our intrinsic entities,

Encompassing these poetic prolific
testimonies of a poetized
viva voce idiom poet and prose writer.

Unleashed Nirvana

Unleashed Nirvana,
to the Outside Realm,
between Reality,
and just Existing,
In the aura of Unleashed Nirvana,
Ensnares me in a whirlwind of hope,
and Unleashed Nirvana.

As I transcribe,
eloquent poetic libretto,
eloquently penned on vellum.

Unleashed Nirvana,
Encloses me in it's grasp.

Beckoning me,
to Unleash Nirvana poetically to the cosmos,
from the Beginning to the End of viva voce idiom,
and poetic expression,

Unleashed Nirvana as yellow as the sun shinning it's glistening light upon us,
to the cosmic realm between Reality and just Existing.

Unleashed Nirvana 2

Unleashed Nirvana,
to the Outside Realm,
between Reality,
and just Existing,

In the aura of Unleashed Nirvana,
Ensnares me in a whirlwind of hope,

As I transcribe,
eloquent poetic libretto,
eloquently penned on vellum.

Unleashed Nirvana,
Encloses me in it's grasp.

Beckoning me,
to Unleash Nirvana poetically to the cosmos,
from the Beginning to the End of viva voce idiom,
and poetic expression,

Unleashed Nirvana as yellow as the sun shinning it's glistening light upon us,
to the cosmic realm between Reality and just Existing.

Happiness Is

Happiness is
what happiness does

Happiness is
what happiness does
It's love, just because

Happiness is
what happiness does
It's what you make it.
It's called love for each other.

I love him

I love him and he loves me,
we can't truly be
but he's my sedusa
and I'm his medusa.

Covered and entwined
in us
I love him and he loves me,
we can't truly be
but he's my sedusa
and I'm his medusa.

In both of our dreams
he lasso's me
I love him and he loves me,
we can't truly be
but he's my sedusa
and I'm his medusa.

Reveal Yourself

Reveal Yourself to me,
Transform me,
Make me whole again,
love me unconditionally.

Show me who you are,
Speak to me
No need to be
afraid of me.

Be honest
with me
reveal your mind, body,
and soul to me.

Maybe just your
mind and soul
to me.

Reveal yourself to me,
and teach me
how to truly love
again me, myself, and I,
and the lord
as one accord
than I can love you more.

My newest Angel

My newest Angel,
Another great strong,
women gone,
in our family

I'll miss you
won't ever forget you,
my beautiful cousin
enough with that
first cousin once removed
.... !
you were my cousin no matter what;
that once removed stuff is confusing anyways.

My newest Angel
my dear sweet cousin Ann
protect me, watch over me
like all the rest of our family
that went before you,
Love you always.

My light 2

"My light"
you are the greatest
gift God has given me.
You are my reason
to be
Without you in my
life,
I cannot shine,
"My light"
I gave you breath,
a beating heart,
beautiful hair,
and beautiful radiant eyes.

"My Light"
forever is you
my child
and will
not ever
change.

Enlightenment 2

" Enlightenment"
I see me
under my skin
trying to peek in,
Silence,
Peaceful bliss,
shines through
Cause my
Enlightenment is in me
Shinning bright as I can be..

Watching you
like an angel
overhead,

You see it in my luminous eyes
Shinning ever so bright
throughout the
Day and Night.

"I'm Enlightenment"
My reason to be,
My life,
My gift,
My song,
My light,
God's given me.
Forever but not
goodnight
the power in me,
Is,Is,
Is,
A Gift from God,
"My Enlightenment is me."

Timeless

Laughter is timeless
Imagination has
NO AGE
Dreams are FOREVER.

So Capture me
through time
and space
so our sacred dreams
can last with us
for forever.

And blast off
in love forever.

Finally

Finally I can see
the stars,
shinning above me

Making me proud
of me
striving to be
the best poetic
woman that I can be

Not settling for
No one
Not giving up '
on my dreams
floating upon
the midnight
sky.

Finally 2

Finally I can see
me,
the best poetic
Kris Jus Me woman
I will be.

Guiding Light 2

Guiding Light,my true light
beyond the glimmering light.
Guiding Light,
yellow as the sun,
Soaring
like an eagle
drifting silently
bye.

You are my
Guiding light
piercing my astral body
trying to see the light,
The Guiding Light.

Guiding Light,
watching you
like an arc angel overhead,

I see it in your era descent eyes,shinning ever so bright
throughout the day and night
shines my Guiding Light.

Guiding Light, see,
how you shimmer and gleam with the slightest touch as you shine unto me.

So you see silence,is the harmonious luxurious bliss that the Guiding light seeks to

find and shines through the Guiding light as strong as can be,
Which causes, Awakening of knowledge to shine upon me like the yellow sun
Shining bright as can be like a Guiding light between you and me,
So you see, I'm the Guiding light that you seek to meet,throughout the day and night.
I inquire thee to see the Guiding light in you throughout the day and night,

And I express to thee will you be my Guiding Light tonight
and throughout the ages?

Alluring Skies

I sit,

I wait,

I watch,

the alluring moon descend

from my blueish skies

within my pulsating abatis

I sit,

I wait,

I watch,

in lieu of my faithful amor to return.

I sit,

I wait,

I watch,

until the sea turns blueish purple

Yo sink to be no more

chained by the muse of Archean

Angelic blueish, purple, and orange butterfly.

I sat,

I waited,

I watched,

until the alluring moon descended

from my blueish skies

shinning bright and gleaming like the sun arose

in the morning sky.

Upon the blueish alluring sky

the stars shine and gleam a never-ending story

across the river of Archeozoic

which has shown an image that looks upon someone's

cardiac muscle to see and envision a mortals true enchantress

pero mi amor nunca aparecio.

My Patch Of Old Snow 2

I sit,
waiting,
Emotions come over me,
Like a thief in the night.

I transform,
myself into my relapsed consciousness
As a little girl scared of expressing
Her true self,

So I transcribe,
my aspirations,Emotions,
Agitations and Tribulations down
upon the past recollected
memories of existence.
Frees me from
my past and my mortal essence,
to be me,
The neverending
changing
Goddess before me.

I am strong,
Free from
my consciousness
Never ending and still.
Memories of me
the patch of old snow a 38 year old.

Disability is in me
but it
doesn't take
over me.
Memories of me the patch of old snow.

The Power Of A Poet

The power of a poet
is
the
words and
mannerisms
in
which one speaks
The way one
Carries themselves
upon the stage
gliding and
changing their
tone
as they speak
Transforming the
audience into the
place that they
speak of
having them hanging
on every word
making them speechless as
the words
Glide effervescently
off their tongues.
I love that feeling
I seem to soar beyond the blueish skies
reaching a poets
destiny even
more
and
more.

The Power Of The Pen

The Power of the Pen transforms all things
to make a change in society.
It can uplift people to a peaceful uprising
It can talk people down
from committing suicide.

So through my Pen
I'll uplift the people whoever felt oppressed,
different or have been bullied into
thinking your not special, beautiful,kind,
powerful, strong Courageous in their fight whether it is

To live another day
striving to make
a way for their family.

The Power of An Artist

The Power of an Artist
combines and
transforms reality
As they put,
the brush to the
Canvas
the paint,
drips d
o
w
n
to make
Something
Magnificent and Magical
which transforms
the piece
into a beautiful
creative
M
A
S
T ER
P I
E
C
E
Making you see
And feel like
You are an Artist
that
Transforms
Time and
Space to
make something new out of Nothing
(A BLANK CANVAS).

Let's Dance

Life to me
is like
a dance
so peaceful and
serene,
just like ballet.

Twirling and gliding
in the air as you
take that giant leap
of faith.

Let's dance
and
soar high into the sky.
Ballet is nice and
smooth
while Tap is
funk and jazzy.

Hip Hop and Go-Go
dancing are the best
to me the beats flow
through me
and makes me
dance and feel the
flow.

Let's not forget
Salsa, Rumba, Marenga
and Rumba dancing
with a sassy sexy flava
all their own.

The Power Of Dance

The music makes
me want to dance.

I feel every beat
inside of me
flowing freely
through me
like a waterfall

So I sway to
the beat
and dance
and move my sensual hips
ever so effervescently,
across the linoleum floor
back and forth
and around
and
around

I dance
like a ballerina
on the linoleum
dance floor
to hip hop
and reggae
and mix it up
with a twist
of hip hop
and ballet mix.

Changing

I'm changing
into a
beautiful butterfly
shedding her skin
to become,
What's within
a Queen
loving herself
Unconditionally.

And trusting someone with,
My whole heart,
without fear
of
Commitment
or without fear of
Abandonment
or without
fear of a man
actually caring about me
Unconditionally.

The Power Of The Mic

The Power of the Mic
in my hand,
transforms me
and
makes me whole
and free again.

The Power of the Mic
is like my air
to breath
it suffocates me
when I'm away
from it.
Making me dread
another day
when I'm not
near it.

It allows me to
escape to a world
of my own
Rebuilding a new
image of me,
into a Queen Poetress.

Poetry and any form
of Artistic Expression are
the Keys to Unlock
my soul,
If you want
me to let you
into it,
My heart,
My soul
will be one with you.

Affirmations

Love
self
and
Others will too.

I am courage.
I am beautiful.
I am intellectual.

I have faith in me.
I am me.
I am strong as can be.

I love, love in it's entirety.
So why not love me
in my entirety?

So I question thee?
To love me throughout eternity.

Caged Bird Once

I once was a caged bird
Singing sweetly and sublime
Lost my voice
but I'm still me,

Still caged in my mind,
And
Spirit
ever so slightly I glide
Unto the highest heights
Every time I write
or
do spoken word,
I feel free unlike a caged bird
flying high amongst the skies.

Building up my might,
to sing and do spoken word again,
To soar like a Nubian Queen.

King

Of course
your my King
my muse
Poetic in verse
and darkness falls
but not for long.

" WE STILL HAVE OUR TWO HEARTS"

Nubian King

Your my Nubian King,
I'm your Nubian Queen
I'm your poet
your amor, and a friend
till the end.

Nubian King
you are
my one true King.

Blossomed love upon my lips
throughout every
kiss
you are a true
God sent gift.

My Nubian King
you are like
a dream
that I've never dreamed before.

Take my hand,
my Nubian King
and,
ride off to the promised land,
together hand in hand
And
love me throughout Eternity.

Nubian Queen

I am your
Nubian Queen
your my Nubian King
Centered
in our joy
and comforted
within your open arms,

Grasping within time
loving every minute
and every hour
of the day
to stay a flight.

I'm your Nubian Queen
who's beautiful,
strong,
and
Resilient
as can be.

Your my Nubian King
who gives me
peace and
makes me
whole and at
peace within
my soul.

My Gift

My Gift is,
a God given gift,
embedded into my soul
Like my own tattoo
That never fades or drifts away.

My gift transforms me and makes me whole,
making me feel free to be me and write my life away

So I can be me and love myself the way God intended me to be,
Creative, strong, free-willed, loveable,
and
huggable as can be.

Vows Of Life

Life has a series
of ups and downs
like a seesaw
highs and lows
or whatever you want to
call it

Don't allow life's struggles
to take a hold
of you and
mold you into
a person that's not the real you.

Live life to the fullest.
Don't be scared of doing things
out of your comfort zone.
Love, Love Unconditionally.

Don't abuse people with brutal words
or tones
Smile and be kind always
Give your heart a chance
always dance to your own rhythm,
and vow to always to help others in need.

Baby Revisited

Baby you are
like a fine wine
to me
Everlasting,
Instilled in me,
Enchanted you are..

As I take a drink of you,
I see the true you
Inside of me.
Enchanted as can be.

All the love you give me
I cherish,
until the end.

Baby Revisited I'm forever sealed with a kiss
Unlike none we both have known before
Your love, lover,
and your friend.

Till we meet again,
the truest you won't
ever end.
And sealed with a kiss
wanting this to never end

" I'll always love you, till we meet again my love"
I'll hope we'll never end".

Stars 2

Soaring,
Drifting,
Falling
upon a
night sky
you.

Drawn to
you.

My stars
shinning,
Soaring,
Dying
in dark nights.

Drifting,
Falling,
Shinning bright

A diamond
glows in a
Moonlight sky.

Your, My
"STAR"
Baby
I'm a
"STAR TOO".

Men Are

Men are handsome
incredible,
loveable,
huggable,
courageous,
and
Strong,
Unbreakable men.

Living the life
trying to survive
"Any means necessary"
is their passionate slogan.
On protecting their wife, lover
and or best friend.

Men are wild beasts
that can be trained or
tamed by love and
compassion,

Some bite while
others value our
pledge over our
selfish fleshy desires.

Women Are

Women are smart
beautiful, positive,
strong,
Courageous and mighty.

Women are,
Confident
fearless
precious
and
extravagant like
a gem or a diamond.

Treat them as
such and
women will
give you the
Key to their
Kingdom OF
Everlasting love,
Grace,
and
Respect
until death do us part.

Take My Hand

Take my hand
and
lead me to the promise land.

Guide my path
and lead me to a
brighter day.

My love where ever
you are hiding
If I am the one
that you seek.

Take my hand
and love me
Unconditionally
No mater what

Hold me
Mold me
Comfort me,
and
Treasure my intellect
and
grasp my soul,
and
my heart
and
take hold of it
Never letting me or it go.

Vow To My Future Husband

The moon
the stars,
and the sun
will align
as I look into your eyes

Making me feel one
with me,
rekindling
our hearts
with one accord

Loving me
Unconditionally
Transforming
time and space
forgiving each
other

And becoming one
one again
not only as poets
but also as lovers
and friends

And maybe one day
something more,
Uniting us as one
Being forever
and ever,

Through everlasting
vows never ending through time.

I AM

I am a woman
beautiful,
and,
strong,
courageous,
and,
strong willed
Cause God made me to be.

I am a Queen
by nature
drifting beyond the sands of time,
from our ancestors past.

Realizing I am not my past.

Blue Skies 2

I see blue skies
shedding away
my
tears and my fears,
every time
I gaze into your
onyx or ochre of your translucent cascading eyes.
They seem to set me into a mesmerizing trance.

No More Makeup

To me true beauty
comes from within.
No more Makeup
is my chant
or
rant.
Not even to hide my
past and present abuse,
scars,
and pain.

No more Makeup,
is my cry
Kris Jus Me's true beauty
illuminates from within
and the
outside cosmic realm.

I'm Worthy

I'm worthy of a man's love.
I used to sit waiting for
a man to tell me,
Your beautiful like the sunrise,
Your spirit is magical,
You make people light up with your smile,

You are perfect the way that you are,
I am worthy of your love
and the,
world's love
" Just Have Faith, in me, and the Lord will, will it to Be."

Waves 2

Waves drifting bye
ever so slightly
beautiful as can be.

Like the pulsating, beating of my myocardium
and
my umbra
everlasting
and
liberated
until the
Raging boisterous
and
mysterious waves
rush over the bluish sea
as the wind picks up
so violently.

Prove To Me

You say your going to prove to me
that
you love me,
How can I you pondered,
Call me everyday,
Love me,
chill with me,

Buy me roses,
Show me that
you care
about me
and
always will be there.

Trust me,
Hold me,
Don't lie on me
Don't try to twist the truth,

Don't control me,
Protect me from harm,
and
Most of all
Don't stop me from achieving my dreams.

Protect Me

I need a man to protect me sometimes,
and
never leave,
me feeling lonely.

Protect me
and
be worthy of me.

Your trust,
Your love,
and Guidance.

Never disrespect me
or
mistreat me in any way.
Never try to control me,

Protect me,till death do us part
with all of your
heart, mind, body,
and soul.

Premonitions or Dreams

Do dreams manifest into premonitions?
I wonder.

Or do they fester and dry up,
Like a raisin in the sun
As my subconscious dream and wither up
and die I pretale.

I've witnessed many subconscious dreams
manifest into premonitions,
the death of two family members
their bodies flew into my atmospheric nature
and
told me they would be OK I'm at peace now

Don't cry over me
We have each other
now to watch over you.

Premonition three was
a sight to envision
what if Trump would win
of course regret that one.
What if he won due to the hacking
low and behold I was right go figure

Do dreams manifest
into premonitions?
I wonder.
Am I weird?
I wonder
Or is this another God given gift
that I succumbed to?
I pretale.

Liberate (Free)

I'm free,
to be me,
every essence of my being is
" Liberated"

You can't control
me
I'm Liberated
from the abuse of you.

Don't you realize you can't break ME NOW?

Liberated means Free
You don't control me
I'm Liberated.